Praise for *You've Got This Baby Brother*

"This is a great book with a phenomenal message."

~Andrew Shapiro: Current Guinness World Record holder for most pull-ups in 6 hours (3,515), 12 hours (5,742), and previously 24 hours (7,306).

"Must read for young children. Gives a wonderful perspective on one of life's most important skills to master - overcoming adversity"

~Cameron Roegner
Former Pitcher: Milwaukee Brewers Organization.

Reading this book genuinely motivated me to use my failures as opportunities. Even though it is intended for kids, adults like me should apply these life skills. Failure is something that should always make us learn and grow and I love that this book preaches that. This is an awesome book for kids in a society that often has a distorted view of success and failure.

~ Alex Marinelli: University of Iowa Wrestler: 3X Big 10 Champion, 3X Academic All-Big Ten: 3X All-American, Team NCAA Champion (2021).

"*You've Got This Baby Brother* is a great read because of its exposure to something that everyone experiences—failure. By teaching kids to embrace the growth that comes from failure, the book is teaching a lifelong lesson in a fun and interactive way."

~ Michael Kemerer: University of Iowa Wrestler: 4 time All-American: 22nd 4X All-American in program history, 4X Academic All-Big Ten, Big 10 Champion, Big Ten sportsmanship award winner, Team NCAA Champion (2021).

"This book has such a great message for young children. I wish I had something like this when I was growing up. It's very important for children to learn to overcome adversity and keep working toward their goals."

~ Isabella D'Aquila
Santa Clara Soccer: 2017-2018 Gatorade National Girls Soccer player of the year, NCAA Champion (2020), USA soccer.

"*You've Got This Baby Brother* teaches kids about one of life's most important lessons in a fun and easy way. A must have staple to add to the book collection."

~ Skylar Killough-Wilhelm: University of Washington Gymnast, Barstool Athlete.

"This book is amazing. An absolute must read!"

~ Gabby Curry: Kentucky Volleyball, NCAA Champion (2020).

"You've Got This Baby Brother brings light to a topic that isn't talked about enough in our younger years: failure. This simple story is the perfect way to introduce one of life's most important lessons to your children."

~ Ally Schlegel: Penn State Soccer.

"The story is super cute! "Understanding that failure opens doors to success is an important lesson for children to learn at a young age. This story helps to eliminate the negative connotation with failure and teaches kids to never give up."

~ Jayda Woods: Georgia Track & Cross Country, Ignite Model MPLS.

YOU'VE GOT THIS BABY BROTHER

You've Got This Baby Brother

Published by 1st World Publishing

P.O. Box 2211, Fairfield, Iowa 52556

tel: 641-209-5000 • fax: 866-440-5234

web: www.1stworldpublishing.com

First Edition

LCCN: Library of Congress Cataloging-in-Publication Data

ISBN Softcover: 978-1-4218-3701-7

While learning to walk,

and learning to talk.

I learned some lessons I wanted to share.

Like how to fail and why you should care.

I had this goal of wanting to walk.

I had this goal of wanting to talk.

FAILURE

I tried and failed,

and tried some more.

That still didn't get me
off the kitchen Floor.

I kept going and going crawling through my defeat.

That is what brought me to my feet.

If you just keep going long enough

eventually something will go your way.

Or at least,

that's what I told myself every day.

Failure doesn't exist to me.

It's all about what you see!

LESSONS

FAILURE = OPPORTUNITY

Victory bell

I see failure as an opportunity.

Every time I fell,

I was just a little bit closer

to ringing the victory bell.

LESSONS

I see failure as something good.

Failure is too often misunderstood.

It helps us learn, and helps us grow.

That's one lesson I want you to know.

So, take your mistakes,
and your failures too,
and let them be
the reason you grew.

If you keep going and growing

in spite of defeat.

Eventually there will be

nothing you can't beat.

Failure is not the enemy.

If you use it wisely

it will set you free.

opportunity

So, keep going and going and never give up,

and sooner than later you'll be able to stand up.

Big Brothers Favorite Quotes

"Failure isn't fatal, but failure to change might be."

~ John Wooden

"Inside of your greatest failures lies your greatest fuel."

~ Garrett Greiner

"You'll win some, you'll lose most. Your ability to flush your mistakes and celebrate your small victories will allow you to grow and be happy."

~ Andrew Shapiro

"Pain + reflection = progress."

~ Ray Dalio

"Success is stumbling from failure to failure with no loss of enthusiasm."

~ Winston Churchill

"Everybody comes to a point in life when they want to quit, but it's what you do at that moment that determines who you are."

~ David Goggins

"Failure is simply the opportunity to begin again, this time more intelligently."

~ Henry Ford

"I never lose. Either I win or I learn."

~ Conor McGregor

"Failure is a necessary experience for growth in our lives."

~ Arnold Schwarzenegger

About the Author

Garrett Greiner is a future Guinness World Record holder and inevitable NYT best-selling author. His confidence comes from his love of writing, his desire to constantly improve his craft, and his willingness to do whatever it takes.

Garrett aspires to be a philanthropist—contributing to the world not just with money, but with joy, wisdom, hope, and a belief in what is possible.

*100% of the proceeds from this book will be donated to the University of Iowa Children's Hospital.

CPSIA information can be obtained
at www.ICGtesting.com
Printed in the USA
LVHW070843151121
703359LV00006B/261